The Lamanites Hide Their Swords

T0272329

written by Tiffany Thomas
illustrated by Nikki Casassa

CFI · An imprint of Cedar Fort, Inc. · Springville, Utah

HARD WORDS:
Lamoni, sword, believe

PARENT TIP: Do not push a child to read
so much that they develop reading fatigue.

King Lamoni and his
people are now good.

King Lamoni
helps his dad
believe.

3

All the good Lamanites are sad.

They do not want to kill anymore.

They put their swords in a big hole.

They tell God they will
never fight again.

The bad Lamanites are mad.

They try to hurt the good Lamanites.

The good Lamanites run away.

The Nephites give them
a new home.

Everyone is happy.

The end.

This is not an official publication of The Church of Jesus Christ of Latter-day Saints. The opinions and views expressed herein belong solely to the author and do not necessarily represent the opinions or views of Cedar Fort, Inc. Permission for the use of sources, graphics, and photos is also solely the responsibility of the author.

ISBN 13: 978-1-4621-4337-5

Published by CFI, an imprint of Cedar Fort, Inc. • 2373 W. 700 S., Suite 100, Springville, UT 84663
Distributed by Cedar Fort, Inc., www.cedarfort.com

Cover design and interior layout design by Shawnda T. Craig
Cover design © 2022 Cedar Fort, Inc.
Printed in China • Printed on acid-free paper
10 9 8 7 6 5 4 3 2 1